# INTRODUCTION

Kumi and Chanti are two African children. They have been given great magical powers and sent on a very special mission. Their mission is to be the caretakers of African-American history. And, they are to take this history to the children of the world.

Kumi is eight, his sister, Chanti is six. They can travel all over the world through space and time. In so doing, they watch and record true stories. Stories about great African-American lives and deeds.

When Kumi and Chanti touch the golden chairs they wear, they can fly. When they sprinkle themselves with their special dust, they can become invisible. When they use their magic twigs, they can change into anything they wish.

Join Kumi and Chanti in their exciting world of African-American history!

This story is about Jean Baptiste DuSable!

"JEAN BAPTISTE DU SABLE"

Published by Empak Enterprises, Inc.
212 East Ohio Street, Chicago, IL 60611

Publisher & Editor: Richard L. Green
Writer: LaVerne C. Johnson
Assoc. Editor: Deborah A. Green
Production: Dickinson & Associates, Inc.
Illustration: Craig Rex Perry

Look at all those furs.
He is really good at trapping.

He is very good
at trading, too!

DuSable laid his heavy pile of fur skins on the ground and sat on them. He was a fur trapper and trader. He was also a pioneer.

With a trading post, he would have a place to sell his fur skins.

And other things as well, Chanti.

DuSable did not seem to care about the swampland or the bad smell. He told his friends, "I will build my trading post here!"

5

Many children do not know that a Black man was the first settler in Chicago.

They will now, Chanti.

6

DuSable's trading post soon grew in importance.
It became the home for many people, and
the Chicago river provided excellent
transportation.

The place where DuSable built his trading post would one day become the city of Chicago. Chicago is now one of the greatest cities in the world!

There are a lot of Black people on this island.

Most of them are slaves. But, there are free Blacks here, too.

Around 1745, Jean Baptiste Pointe DuSabl was born in the country of Haiti. Hi beautiful Black mother had been a slave His father was said to have been French sea captair

When he was of school age, DuSable's father took him to France to go to school. He became well educated. He learned to speak English, French, and Spanish.

Does DuSable want to go back to Haiti or France?

No, Chanti, he wants to go to America.

As a young man, DuSable was over six feet tall and very strong. He became a seaman on his father's boats.

At the age of 20, on a trip to New Orleans,
DuSable's boat was wrecked and it sank. DuSable
was hurt, but he managed to reach safety.

14

DuSable made his way to New Orleans, but
there was trouble. Some thought that he was
an escaped slave. The priests hid him until he
was well enough to get away.

DuSable left New Orleans. He traveled up the Mississippi River to St. Louis, Missouri. Later, he settled in Peoria, Illinois. And, he quickly made friends with the Potawatomi Indians who lived there.

17

18

DuSable began trading with the Indians.
He learned their customs and often met with
leaders of the Indian tribes.

19

With his Potawatomi wife, Catherine, DuSable settled in Peoria and built his log cabin. They had a daughter, Suzanne, and a son, Jean. DuSable soon owned over 800 acres of land.

DuSable's business often took him as far away as Canada. The only roads were Indian trails, but he was safe.

Every time he went to Canada or Michigan, he had to pass through Chicago. He knew that it would be just the right place for his trading post.

21

1779, DuSable built a large
use and a trading post on
North bank of the
icago River. They
re the first buildings to
built in Chicago.

DuSable's trading post was more than just one building. There was a bakehouse, a dairy, a smokehouse, poultry house, workshop, stable, barn, horsemill, and more.

His trading post was very busy. He sold supplies to White trappers, traders, woodsmen, the Indians, and to other trading posts.

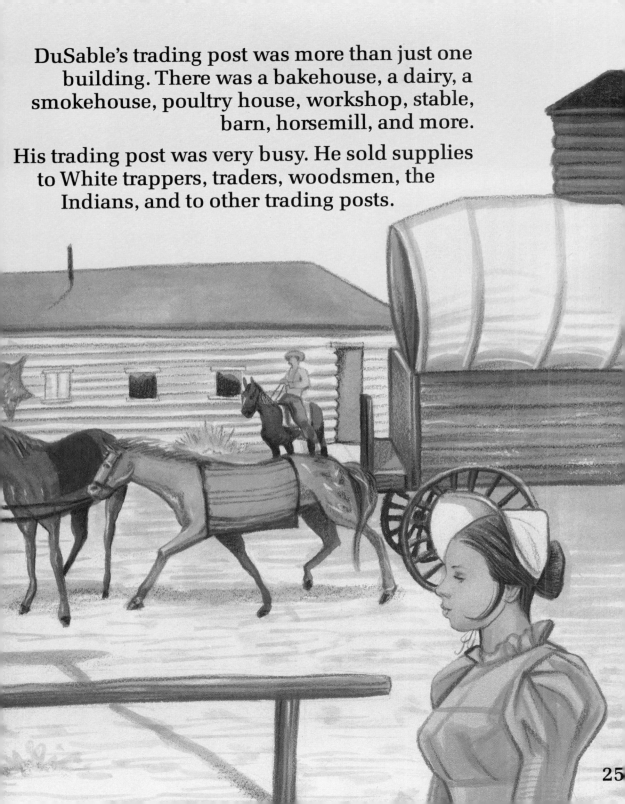

It's nice that the family is together again, Kumi.

In 1784, DuSable sent for his family. His daughter was married in Chicago. And his granddaughter became the first child to be born in Chicago.

26

27

Important buildings now stand where DuSable and the Indians once traded.

The land that he once owned is now worth a fortune, Chanti.

DuSable, the great pioneer, died 18 years after he left Chicago. Most of his money was gone. He was buried in St. Charles, Missouri.

Jean Baptist Pointe DuSable saw more than the "land of bad smells" when he picked the right place for his trading post. He saw a great city.

Many books have been written about DuSable. And, many schools and museums throughout the country are named in his honor. Chicago has two city plaques in honor of him. One plaque is in the Chicago Historical Society. The other is at the Michigan Avenue bridge.

In 1968, the State of Illinois and the City of Chicago named DuSable the "Father of Chicago." Later in 1986, a postage stamp was issued in his name by the federal government.

JEAN BAPTISTE POINTE
DUSABLE